I know what time it is! It's s
You, God, for spring!

MELISSA BLUE/PHOTOGRAPH BY DAVID H. AHRENHOLZ, M.D.

A Special Time of Year

A BOOK ABOUT JOY

Sharon Lee Roberts
Illustrated by Susan Nethery

Chariot Books™
David C. Cook Publishing Co.

Chariot Books™ is an imprint of David C. Cook Publishing Co.
David C. Cook Publishing Co., Elgin, Illinois 60120
David C. Cook Publishing Co., Weston, Ontario
A SPECIAL TIME OF YEAR
©1990 David C. Cook Publishing Co. All rights reserved.
Cover and interior design by Dawn Lauck
First Printing, 1990. Printed in the United States of America.
95 94 93 92 91 90 5 4 3 2 1
ISBN 1-55513-359-2 LC 89-62110

Know what time it is? It's a special time. . . .

It's time to put away my red wool coat with the black buttons and start wearing my sky blue sweater.

It's time to put my ice skates away and ask Dad to oil my roller skates. It's time to open the windows and let the crisp fresh air come in from outside.

Have you had enough clues yet? No? It's time for the crocuses to pop up their silky purple heads around the well in my front yard.

It's time for the first robin to show off
his red velvet breast as he perches on the
dogwood tree outside my bedroom
window and sings me his prettiest song.

It's time for the days to last a little
longer as the sun smiles down on the earth.

Do you know what time it is yet?
It's time for the shiny green frogs to
hippity-hop around the pond as they talk
to each other with a "ribbet-ribbet,
croak-croak!"

Have you guessed yet?
It's time to watch for furry little
bunnies with warm pink noses . . .

and little yellow chicks
hatching from their eggs—
peek-a-boo!

It's time to see butterflies spread their delicate wings as they break forth from their cocoons.

But most important, it's time to
remember that wonderful miracle
when Jesus rose, after the Cross, to
live in heaven and in our hearts for
ever and ever—
Your heart and mine.

IT'S *EASTERTIME!*